YOUR KNOWLEDGE HAS VALUE

- We will publish your bachelor's and master's thesis, essays and papers

- Your own eBook and book - sold worldwide in all relevant shops

- Earn money with each sale

Upload your text at www.GRIN.com
and publish for free

Imprint:

Copyright © 2015 GRIN Verlag, Open Publishing GmbH
Print and binding: Books on Demand GmbH, Norderstedt Germany
ISBN: 9783668410732

This book at GRIN:

http://www.grin.com/en/e-book/350643/comparing-and-contrasting-caribbean-african-american-and-black-south-african

Dexx Rose

Comparing and contrasting Caribbean, African American and Black South African feminist strategies

GRIN Publishing

Gender, Political Activism and Mobilization

Comparing and contrasting Caribbean feminist strategies (past and present) to those employed by African American and black South African Women in their respective movements.

For the last two decades women have organized movements against violent institutions that oppress them. They created simple strategies and bonds that brought them together through their shared and lived experiences and have come to challenge political, cultural and historical policies that oppress women. With the rise of different feminist branches worldwide such as; Caribbean feminism, African American feminism and Black South African feminism, women began to rely on each other for support and strength to challenge the institutional notion of patriarchy that they were subjected to. Black feminism exploded in the 1960s in response to gendered issues and racism that stemmed from the civil rights movement. "Problematising race and exposing how racist practices complicate all other social relations of power is a central organising principle of black feminist theorising" (Barriteau, 2003). While these three branches of feminism developed in different time periods and differ in theory and objectives, the strategies used and implemented by women in these movements are quite similar.

The Caribbean, like other parts of the world has been cultured and shaped by racial constructs and ideologies, due to its history. 'Race' according to Professor Reddock may be defined as socially constructed groupings differentiated by phenotype, physical features and area of origin. "The Caribbean is often linked with the emergence of racism, which could be dated back to its encounter between Europe, Africa and the New World" (Reddock, 2007). Caribbean feminists have played a very important role in deconstructing the categories of race and expressing the relationship between gender and race. In the early twentieth century Caribbean feminist addressed "women who were conscious of their African and Indian heritage at a time of great European colonial power" (Reddock, 2007). Who then are Caribbean feminists and what is Caribbean feminism? Barriteau explains that, by describing herself as a Caribbean feminist she defines herself "as a black woman, a feminist and a political scientist, who reflects upon and negotiates, operates, theorises, and works within the trenches of gender relations in the Commonwealth Caribbean." Like many other branches of feminism, Caribbean feminism aims to challenge patriarchal dominance in the Caribbean, increase the visibility of women and make for a more inclusive society regardless of race and gender.

Caribbean history is closely related to the history of racism itself, with "European conquest of the region, introduction of forced labour systems leading to the eventual decimation of the indigenous peoples" (Barriteau, 2003). This is an important point to note, as Caribbean feminism is built on a foundation of history, with the work of scholars such as Lucille Mathurin Mair, whose thesis has played an important part in Caribbean feminism. "The establishment of the modern slave trade and enslavement of Africans, the importation of bonded labour of Asian and other nationalities were all justified by a Eurocentric discourse of natural racial and cultural superiority." (Reddock, 2007). Reddock also explained that "colonial processes and discourse therefore served to construct 'race' and 'racism' as central organising principles of Caribbean life, traditions and ideology, manifest in the economy, society, culture and social, sexual and gender relations. Through various strategies, Caribbean feminists have contributed significantly across the regions towards deconstructing the categories of 'race.' One strategy was the formation of different women led organizations around the Caribbean such as; Dawn in 1985, Pan- African Association (PAA) in the 1900s, the Committee of Women for Progress (CWP), The Committee for Development of Women in St.Vincent and the Grenadines (CDW) along with Concerned Women for Progress (CWP), The Democratic Women's Association in Trinidad and Tobago and later Red Thread in Guyana. These organizations created a space for women to not only voice their issues, but work toward resolving them. Caribbean feminists also occupied positions in the United Nations and UNICEF, among others. Some of these women who identified as Caribbean feminists included; Amy Bailey, Gema Ramkeesoon, Amy Ashwood, Una Marson, Audre Lorde, Patricia Mohammed and Lucille Mathurin Mair. These women formed a bond of sisterhood, which allowed them to work more strategically in exposing the agency and urgency surrounding Caribbean women and their concerns.

Although it was indeed evident that central themes in Caribbean feminism included race and gender, there were several critiques of Caribbean feminist theorists. One such critique is from Hilary Beckles, as he charges that Caribbean feminist theorists have failed to look at why "institutional political projects such as independence took hegemonic precedence over women's liberation." Rawwida Baksh-Sodeen also critiqued Caribbean feminism as "afrocentric and argues that the women's movement should reflect the experiences of women of other ethnic groups in the region." However the neglecting of issues facing women of other ethnic groups were "possibly because the race and colour discrimination which Afro-Caribbean women faced overshadowed their relations with women of other ethnic groups which were not considered problematic at that time" (Reddock 2007). What is indeed clear is that issues of gender and race were central to the work and consciousness of the early feminist in the Caribbean.

On the other hand African American feminism can be dated back to the nineteenth century when African American feminists such as Maria Stewart and Anna Julia Cooper "challenged the conventions and tradition of their time to openly speak against slavery and in support of rights for black women. African American feminists have always been aware of the impact of race, and gender oppression upon their lives, which could once again be dated back to slavery, as African Americans, like other marginalized black feminists have struggled individually and in groups, to eradicate the multiple injustices they face within their communities. In the early 1800s, most black women were enslaved, however free black women participated in the abolitionist cause. Dedicated women such as Maria Stewart, Frances E.W. Harper, and Sojourner Truth among others, spoke out about Black women's rights. Professor Taylor in his article, "African American Experience" explained that "Sojourner Truth was active in the women's right movement, and her oft-quoted 1851 'Aint I a Woman' speech" which highlighted the ways in which gender oppression had serious repercussions for Black women living in a racist environment.

By the end of the nineteenth century, African American feminists had strategized movements, which were similar to that of the Caribbean feminist movement. According to Professor Taylor, American African feminists had organized their own networking spaces. Some of the issues that were looked at in these spaces supported woman suffrage, but prioritized a range of social and political issues that affected Black communities, as well as black women specifically. Another strategy which African American feminists employed was the use of traditional media. This method was also employed in the Caribbean feminist movements. African American feminism was seen as one of the most radical form of feminism, because of their activism, strategies, involvement and their overall theories, in comparison to that of any other branch of black feminism. Black women's involvement in the civil rights movements during the 1950s and 1960s was very beneficial and rather crucial to women's movements at the time. It facilitated grounds for public discourse on the oppression of the black woman in both the private and public sphere, which Caribbean feminists played an active role in.

As time continued, African American discourse started to include not only issues of race and gender, but also the issue of black women's sexuality and challenging the idea of black women as immoral and loose. "African American feminists for the first time began to question the reality of sexual oppression within the black community as well as how the sexism in the society as a whole impacted them as black women." (Hassim, 1991).This was something that had not been explored initially by other branches of feminism. Until this day, African American feminism, rooted in its struggles of generations of black women, continues to play a vital role in the socio-political life of the United States. As they continue to redefine women, black men and what it means to be a sexual being, they also continue to challenge homophobia in the black community and fight for the reproductive rights of women.

Like other branches of feminism, Black South African feminism stemmed from an urgency to end patriarchal dominance in South Africa and end racism. "Black women in South Africa were uniquely oppressed because theirs is a three-fold oppression as blacks, as workers and as women" (Hassim 1991). Black South African feminists explored and capitalized on opportunities to gain visibility to women's oppression. This type of feminism later changed its focus from involving gender in the discussion of race and women's oppression to women's protection and resistance. It is said by many historians that Black South African feminism shifted their focus to structure and agency. "Scholars associated with the Wit History Workshop and the School of Oriental and African Studies (SOAS) in particular contributed to the limited but growing recognition that feminist perspectives had value, that to analyse gender, and to acknowledge the politics of the ' domestic,' might enrich our understanding the race/class nexus" (Clowes & Spuy, 2007).

In addition to that, Black South African feminism academics were drawn into key debates concerning African feminisms in the face of western feminist imperialism.

"Perhaps ironically, western feminist insistence on authorial subjectivities thus became a critical aspect of South African feminist concerns, and began to become evident in publication (Clowes & Spuy, 2007). Clowes & Spuy in their article "Accidental Feminist" further explored that strategies that involved traditional media spaces can be seen across the different waves of feminism that are explored in this piece; this was used as an activism tool to capture and secure a space for women's voices and empowerment, through creating women led spaces. In Black South African Feminism scholarship was definitely important, and was a key strategy used by feminist women of the time in South Africa. "The first book of essays specifically dealing with the history of women and gender in Southern/South Africa was Cheryl Walker's 1990 edited volume, Women and Gender in Southern Africa to 1945." As scholars often looked at 'the indigenous and the settler sex-gender systems,' the unifying forces of colonialism and capitalism, of the settler over the indigenous and also 'gender oppression in Southern Africa's precapitalist societies were all important to the discussions and theories surrounding Black South African feminist.

Black South African feminism had a focus on structure and agency "Within South African historiography, question concerning the relationship between (south) African feminism and women's histories and the impact of transnational, African, and local feminist theory and scholarship continues to be felt unevenly (Clowes & Van Der Spuy). Black South African feminism has attracted several critiques as a feminist movement. One such critique is that; there is a bit of confusion surrounding the movement and about how to explain women's oppression in contemporary South Africa (Walker 1990). Walker also explained that there was a lack of emphasis on the relationship between gender and women's oppression, when indeed it was very important to have a gendered analysis of its society. They were also critiqued for the heavy Marxist influence that was obvious in their literature, as this made them seem as if they were not inclusive enough. Despite the critiques, Black South African feminism has helped the feminist discourse and continues to do so through scholar activism.

Women from the different regions, whether they identified themselves as feminist, or were defined in literature as feminist have made a great impact in the Caribbean, South Africa and America. While these branches of feminism share similarities, scholars have noted significant difference in the movements. For instance, it is said that Caribbean feminism is a very practical form of feminism and grounded in the unique experiences of Caribbean women. While history is undoubtedly important in the foundation of both black South African and African American feminism, history is a critical tool used in both the foundation and development of Caribbean feminism. Caribbean feminist looks at how men's involvement in empowering women is critical, men and women have shared history. This ensures that Caribbean feminism is one of the most inclusive branches of feminism, with its activism surrounding violence against women, male involvement, and homophobia, all from a gendered, historical perspective.

It can be argued that other feminist movement such as the Black South African and African American movements are involved with women ad their oppression, and therefore ignore men and neglect to include them in these movements. It was not until later that they started taking a more gendered approach to their theories while this was something Caribbean feminists had been doing from the start. While African American feminists have recently opened the discourse board to facilitate a more gendered discussion, it was not always so.

Although the tactics were different in some instances, the overall strategy applied by these aspects of feminism were very similar, Caribbean feminism, African American and Black South African strategies employed the use of activism, scholars and capturing spaces in influential, global organizations as a way to promote and facilitate discussions surrounding women's oppression and other gendered discourse. These strategies governed the rising of the black feminist movements and continue to play a very important role in highlighting the agency and urgency of gender issues in the Caribbean, America and South Africa.

Today, although we have indeed come along way, there is still much work that needs to be done in the Caribbean, South Africa and America where feminism is concerned. There is a need for more focus on mainstreaming gender in different sectors and narratives. Work also needs to be done to help to write literature from a more gendered perspective, especially looking at men and how they are important to development. Strategies from the past have been effective and important towards the different feminist movements. However for all three branches of feminism, more recent strategies, such as social media campaigns and the use of social media spaces should be employed in order to attract attention and shed light on some of the issues that face women in today's society, such as institutional oppression, gender-based violence and sexual violence. Through these old and new strategies, we can continue to create visibility for women's issues and modern day oppression.

References

Baksh- Soodeen R. (1998) "Issues of Difference in Contemporary Caribbean Feminism," Feminist Review 59, No.1, 74-85.

Barriteau, E. (2003). 'Conclusion: beyond a Blacklash- the frontal assault on containing Caribbean women in the decade of the 1990s' in Nain, G.T. and Bailey, B. (2003) editors, Gender Equality in the Caribbean: Reality or Illusion, Jamaica: Ian Randle and CARICOM, 201-232.

French, Joan and Honor Ford-Smith. *Women, Work and Organization in Jamaica: 1990-1944*, Research Report, The Hague: Institute of Social Studies, 1985.

Hassim, S. (1991) Gender, Social Location and Feminist Politics in South Africa.

Reddock, R. (2007). Diversity, Difference and Caribbean Feminism: The Challenge of Anti- Racism. Journal of Caribbean Perspectives on Gender and feminism, 1, 15-21.

Schneir, M. ed. 1972. Feminism: The essential Historical Writings. New York: Vintage Books.

Smith, B. ed. (1993). Home Girls: A Black Feminist Anthology. Kitchen Table Women of Color Press: New York.

Spuy, P. & Clowes, L. (2007). Accidental Feminists? Recent Histories of South African Women. Retrieved from http:// www. Jstor.org/stable/41056589.

Taylor, Q. (2000). The African American Experience: A History of Black Americans from 1619 to 1890. University of Washington.

Vassell, L. (2003. "Women, Power and Decision-Making in CARICOM Countires: Moving forward from a Post-Beijing Assessment" in Tang Nain, Gemma and Bailey, Barbara. Eds. Gender equality in the Caribbean: Reality or Illusion? Kingston: Ian Randle Publishers

Walker, C. (1982). Women and Resistance in South Africa. London: Onyx.

YOUR KNOWLEDGE HAS VALUE

- We will publish your bachelor's and master's thesis, essays and papers

- Your own eBook and book - sold worldwide in all relevant shops

- Earn money with each sale

Upload your text at www.GRIN.com and publish for free